Eleanor Baillon

Life of Saint John of God

Eleanor Baillon

Life of Saint John of God

ISBN/EAN: 9783741160073

Manufactured in Europe, USA, Canada, Australia, Japa

Cover: Foto ©Andreas Hilbeck / pixelio.de

Manufactured and distributed by brebook publishing software (www.brebook.com)

Eleanor Baillon

Life of Saint John of God

LIFE

OF

SAINT JOHN OF GOD.

BY
ELEANOR BAILLON.

———:o:———

London:
THOMAS RICHARDSON AND SON;
23, King Edward Street, City;
and Derby.
DUBLIN: M. H. GILL AND SON,
50, Upper Sackville Street.

PREFACE.

THE Order of the Brothers of Saint John of God, known too as "Fratres Hospitalitatis," "Fate bene fratelli," or "Frères de la Charité," was founded in Spain in the sixteenth century, and was approved by Pope S. Pius V., in 1572, by Pope Sixtus V., in 1586, and confirmed by Pope Paul V., in 1617.

Saint John of God, the founder of this Religious Institute, was born in Montemor-o-nova, in Portugal, in the year 1495. In his fortieth year he was drawn strongly to God's service, and began a wonderful life of prayer, penance, and charity towards his neighbour. Pressed by love of God and man, he founded two hospitals in the city of Granada, where he tenderly served the sick and poor. While thus employed he received the Religious habit, and unwittingly laid the foundation of the Order that was to bear his name. After ten years, spent in works of heroic charity, he fell sick, and on the 8th of March, 1550, died on his knees before the altar. He was canonized by Pope Alexander VIII., in 1690, and is commemorated in the Roman Martyrology on the anniversary of his holy death. The rule of his Order, based on that of Saint Augustine, was drawn up six years after his death, but Religious vows were only introduced into it in 1570.

The Brothers, after the example of their holy Founder, seek, with their own sanctification, their neighbour's spiritual and temporal welfare, but chiefly the good of the sick, and infirm, and poor. To the three solemn vows of Religion they add a fourth, of serving the sick and poor for life.

The Order is governed by a Prior-General, who resides in Rome, and is composed of laymen, though priests desiring to devote their sacred ministry to the Brethren and the patients are received. The members live in Hospital-Convents, under a Prior, where they spend their time in serving the sick, and in performing the usual duties and pious exercises of Religious life. The members assist together daily at Holy Mass, prayers, and meditation, the recital of the Office of our Lady, spiritual reading, meals, and recreation.

Before the evil days that came with the end of the last century, the Order was widely spread throughout the world. Even now it counts its 101 Hospital-Convents, 1179 Brethren, of whom 75 are Priests, 58 Graduates in Surgery, 14 Graduates in Medicine and Surgery, and 78 Certificated Apothecaries. It directs Hospitals for the Sick and for

Incurables, Dispensaries, Asylums for Lunatics, Homes for the Old and Helpless. The "Maison de Sainté," Rue Oudinot, Paris, whither gentlemen come from all parts of Europe to have their diseases treated, is one of the Houses of the Order. In some provinces hospices have been opened for aged and infirm priests, while elsewhere the Brethren have the care of military hospitals, and in time of war devote themselves to the succour of the wounded in ambulances, even accompanying for this end the troops upon the field of battle. The Houses of the Order are supported by endowments, by yearly grants from Governments, Corporations, or Societies, by voluntary alms and subscriptions, by the pension paid by patients, and by the labour and questing of the Brethren.

The following synopsis gives the state of the Order at the present day:—

Provinces.	Convents.	Brethren.	Beds in Hospitals.
1. Roman	14	108	1076
2. Lombardo-Venetian	12	94	857
3. Neapolitan	8	31	517
4. Sicilian	4	12	—
5. French	9	268	3316
6. Austro-Bohemian	19	266	1012
7. Bavarian	9	88	428
8. Prussian	6	95	381
9. Hungarian	14	165	740
10. Spanish	4	45	94
11. American	2	7	94

Although the Polish Convents have been suppressed, yet has the Order been in some way compensated by the foundation of Houses in the United States of America, and in Buenos Ayres; besides two Houses have been lately established in Ireland; one of them is near

Dublin, S. Patrick's, for invalid gentlemen.

In October, 1880, a Hospital was founded in Yorkshire, at Scorton, near Catterick. The climate is exceptionally healthful, the subsoil being so gravelly, and the air pure. The Hospital has been founded as a home for the aged, the infirm, and for convalescents. Those in easy circumstances are expected to pay something, but the very poor are supported by voluntary contributions. Thus the voice of S. John of God is now to be heard in England and Ireland crying out, as of old in the streets of Granada, "Brethren, do good to yourselves, do good to yourselves, in giving to the poor." The Hospital at Scorton will hold a hundred inmates, but how far it is to be filled must depend in a measure on the generosity with which the charitable shall fill the outstretched hand of S. John.

S. John of God.

CHAPTER I:

> "Who art thou that wouldst grave thy name
> Thus deeply in a brother's heart?
> Look on this Saint, and learn to frame
> Thy love-charm with true Christian art."
> KEBLE.

HIGH-SOUNDING names are greatly coveted and sought after by the children of this world. But of all the titles that have ever been borne by king or victor, none has been so magnificent as the one bestowed on this humble servant of the poor by our Lord Himself, when He addressed him by the name of John of God. Under this title was he known in his lifetime, and under the same name will he be for ever honoured in the Church throughout Christendom.

On the 8th of March, in the year 1495, the inhabitants of the town of Montemor-o-nova were startled on hearing the church bells ring at an unwonted hour. They hastened to see what was the matter. Angelic hands, however, had set the bells in motion, and the people returned wonder-struck at the occurrence. The mysterious ringing was followed by another marvel; a fiery light was seen hovering over the modest dwelling of Andrew Ciudad, a devout man, whose wife had just given birth to a son. Then said the astonished people one to another, "What will this child be, whose entrance into life is marked by signs so wonderful?" The little one received the name of John, and from his early years he gave himself to God. When he was eight years old he left his home in the company of a priest to whom his pious parents had offered hospitality. What the motive of his flight was has not been explained by the chroniclers of his life. But may he not, like the fiery-hearted Teresa, have been moved by an inner impulse to obey the call of God? He, however, was not overtaken and brought back home. His mother died some days after his disappearance, and his father became a Franciscan friar. John journeyed on as far as the town of Oropesa, in Castile. Here, having no means of subsistence, he tended sheep under the chief shepherd of the Count of Oropesa.

The life of a shepherd is conducive to prayer and contemplation. Lonely communing with nature is of itself sufficient to lift the mind from things earthly to things which are above. When John had led the flocks to pasture, he gave himself up to meditation, for he had great delight in prayer. He had a tender devotion to our Lady, and it was his daily custom to recite twenty-four Pater's and Ave's in honour of the twenty years she spent on earth after the ascension of her Divine Son. In all things mild and gentle, we are told that self-love was John's leading fault in his youth.

At this period Europe was made the theatre of continual scenes of bloodshed, owing to the jealousy of two rival monarchs, Francis I. of France, and Charles V. of Germany. War was declared by the French king, to recover Navarre,* which Charles had taken. A military levy was raised in Spain, and in 1522 John took up arms in her cause. Gouvea, a chronicler of the Saint's life, describes him at this time as being tall, robust, and wearing a dark beard, his vigorous appearance testifying that he

* It was during this campaign, at the siege of Pampeluna, that S. Ignatius received the happy wound which was the cause of his becoming so eminent a soldier of Jesus Christ.

was more suited for the brilliant career of a soldier than that of a simple shepherd.

The camp was in those lawless days no likely place to foster the seeds of fervour and piety; and John, after a youth of singular holiness, now became a profligate in the midst of careless-living comrades. He grew from bad to worse, and led a life of unbridled wickedness, his impetuosity drawing him into every excess of vice. He was not, however, devoid of valour. The soldiers of his troop being once in want of food, John offered to seek for something to relieve their hunger. Mounting a horse without saddle or bridle, he rode on to the very skirts of the enemy's camp. The horse suddenly plunging, John was thrown among some rocks. For two hours he lay unconscious, and on coming to himself, although suffering great bodily torture, his greatest dread was of being found and taken prisoner. In his heart there rose the memory of Mary, to whom, as an innocent youth, he had so often addressed his prayers. He fell upon his knees, and entreated our Lady of Compassion to aid him in his peril. Scarcely was his prayer ended than he beheld a lady of unspeakable beauty, in the garb of a shepherdess, standing near to him. She held a drink to his thirsty lips, and after tasting it he felt his strength revive. Dazzled by this vision of unearthly glory, he asked the lady her name. "I am," she replied, "the one whose aid you have just asked. In midst of so many perils you are not safe unless you have recourse to prayer." Having said these words, the vision vanished.

This apparition of our Lady so touched the poor soldier's heart that he again fell insensible. The Mother of Compassion, however, had not come only to aid him in his dangers, but whilst healing his body, she gave a wound to the spirit, and when John recovered his senses, he felt smitten with remorse for his wickedness, and resolved to return to his former practices of devotion. On coming back to his comrades they marvelled to find how completely he was changed. The Lover of souls had knocked at the door of his heart, and John had risen to open to Him. From henceforth the ribald song fell no more from his lips, evil practices were forsaken, and he did his best to regain the lost path of virtue. His companions in sin now only mocked at him. This brought about his dismissal from the camp; for, being left in charge of some booty which, either through carelessness on his part, or theft on that of his comrades, was carried off, he was condemned to death for his negligence. The sentence, however, was not carried into execution, but John was ordered to leave the troop.

He bent his steps towards Oropesa, where amid the tranquil meadows he had spent so many prayerful hours. His former master took him again into his service. In the outer man there was no change in John. The change was in his heart, and was a secret between God and himself. Having given himself to the pleasures of sin for a time, he had forfeited his former peaceful state of mind, and he had to endure a most fearful combat against his spiritual foes. Anxiety had taken the place of peace, and bitter remorse now filled that heart which was once inundated with heavenly delights. His hands dropped with myrrh, the bitterness thereof filling his soul for ten long years.

Soliman the Magnificent, anxious to extend the glory of the Ottoman name, had, in the year 1529, entered Hungary with fire and sword. The country was ravaged, and the horde of Turkish invaders soon pitched their tents beneath the walls of Vienna. The advance of the dreaded crescent caused Christendom to tremble, and, with all the enthusiasm of those days, men joyfully girded on the sword, and the flower of chivalry hastened to shed its blood in the holy war against the infidel power of the east.

When the news of the atrocities perpetrated by the Turks reached the ears of John, his heart throbbed with indignation, and for the second time he exchanged the shepherd's crook for the soldier's lance. Under the venerable banner of Castile he was found fighting at the siege of Vienna. The city was happily saved, and the Spanish soldiers returned to their own country. John's troop being disbanded, he entered the service of a rich lady living near

Seville, as a shepherd. But he found that he had lost all taste for the pastoral life. He had seen much of human misery, and he now yearned to spend his time in succouring the poor and sinful. God was inflaming his heart with that wonderful spirit of compassion for the suffering which John displayed in so pre-eminent a degree to the end of his life. "Sacrifice" was henceforward to be the watchword of our saint.

CHAPTER II.

"In Afric's foreign land,
   Sweet oil and wine for wounded heart
Didst thou in-pour with gentle hand,
   And mercy's healing art."

ONLY those who have been defiled by the unclean spot of sin can know of the intense sense of gratitude which fills the pardoned sinner's heart.

It is not felt immediately after conversion; it springs from the gradual softening of the heart, and increases with the soul's growth in holiness. God's mercy is to her as a second redemption, and she is filled with a yearning to make reparation for the hateful past.

It was this longing which gave birth in John's heart to a desire to seek for martyrdom in Africa. His compassion was aroused for Christian slaves cruelly treated by Moorish pirates. This led him to leave Seville with the intention of embarking for Barbary, that he might there succour those in captivity. At Gibraltar he met with a Portuguese nobleman condemned to exile by order of the king; he, with his wife and children, were going on board a vessel bound for Ceuta, the place of banishment. John offered his gratuitous services to the unfortunate family, which were gladly accepted. Arriving in Ceuta, they all fell grievously sick, their faithful servant tending them with the utmost devotion. Reduced as they were to indigence, it became necessary for John to maintain them by his labour; he therefore went daily to work at the fortifications of the town, thus earning sufficient to buy bread for the support of the family. It was always to this self-denying charity that the Saint attributed his subsequent graces. The apostacy of a fellow-labourer caused such grief to John's sensitive heart that his confessor advised him to return to Spain, his love of obedience overcoming his reluctance to leave the unhappy exiles. While crossing the Mediterranean a terrible storm arose. John imagined it was sent by God in punishment of his abandonment of his work of charity. He publicly accused himself of his sins, and begged to be thrown into the sea; but after he had recited an Ave Maria the tempest suddenly ceased.

Coming back to Gibraltar, and anxious to devote himself to the service of his neighbour, John now spent the little money he had in buying books and pictures of devotion, which he carried about for sale. How pleasing this was to God the following beautiful incident will show.

As the Saint was once journeying in the country with a pack on his back, Jesus appeared to him under the disguise of a little child. John did not at first recognize Him, but seeing that He was walking barefoot, his tender heart suggested to him to offer his own shoes to his companion. As they could be be made in no way to fit, John lifted the little One on his shoulders. The additional weight almost overwhelmed him, and with gentle hand the Child wiped away the drops of perspiration which were stealing down his face. Seeing a fountain at a little distance, he left his Burden under the shadow of a tree while he went to quench his thirst. On his return the Divine Infant offered him a pomegranate. As John took it the fruit opened, and from it there sprang forth a cross. Then said Jesus, in loving accents, "John of God, at Granada thou wilt find thy cross." Saying this, He disappeared, leaving the Saint inundated with delight. In memory of this apparition the Brothers have adopted as the device of their Order an open pomegranate surmounted by a cross, with the motto, "Granada will be thy cross." From the time of this vision John of God always went barefoot.

For a long time Granada had remained under the dominion of the Moors; but in 1492 it had been taken from them by King Ferdinand. Owing to the insubordination of the Mussulmans, the King obliged them to quit the city. The greater number left, and those who remained made profession of being Christians, but were so only in name. Thus the magnificent city of Granada was left poor and deserted, save by those who were in no way remarkable for the morality of their lives. The city was built on two hills, the plain between being watered by the Darro. The gorgeous palace of the Alhambra rested, like a jewelled crown, on the summit of one of the lofty hills; on its rival there rose marble dwellings, adorned with fountained courts and sunny gardens, where pomegranates, oranges, and citrons, were blended in rich profusion. The whole landscape of hill and grove was enchanting to the eye. So beautiful indeed it was, and so serene the air, that the Moors fancied that the Prophet dwelt in that part of heaven which overlooked this garden of delights. Here it was God's will to call His servant to dwell, and in the year 1538 he opened a shop, for the sale of pious books, in the most frequented part of the city.

We now come to an event in the Saint's life, which has been criticised by many as an extravagant act. Those who find fault with the deeds of the Saints, are generally wanting in the virtues which prompted their execution. What is considered folly by worldlings, is often wisdom before God. After the Saint's death, this event was made a reproach to his memory. John of Avila, and Louis of Granada, however, scorned the imputation. The latter said that those who reproached the Saint were ignorant of that intensity of contrition with which certain favoured souls are filled.

Outside Granada there was a hermitage, dedicated to S. Sebastian; here his feast was kept with great solemnity, and a sermon was preached in the hermitage. On the festival, in 1539, the celebrated John of Avila was to make the panegyric of the martyr: crowds flocked to hear him, and with them came John of God. The preacher's words of fire fell on the ears of the Saint with consuming power. His sins and ingratitude appeared in all the awful clearness of a vision, and he then comprehended, as he had never done before, the hatefulness of sin. He was so affected that tears fell in torrents from his eyes, and he filled the place with his lamentations. As one beside himself with grief, he ran about tearing his hair, and besmearing his face with dirt. The spectators, not understanding the motive of such strange behaviour, followed him with the cry of "Madman." Heedless of their jeers,

John only desired to make public reparation for the past, and falling at the feet of John of Avila, he made a general confession. The holy confessor discovered in his penitent many extraordinary graces and much virtue, and he at once consented to take him under his direction. From this hour these two souls were knit to one another in the bonds of holy friendship. If John of Avila appeared at times to be harsh or severe in his direction, we find his affection for his spiritual son peeping out amidst the apparent sternness. His reply to the Saint's apology for the length of a letter he was sending to him, bears witness to this. "Never fear," he writes, "letters can never be too long between those who love one another."

After making his confession, John, desirous of still greater humiliations, behaved anew in the same seemingly extravagant fashion, feigning complete madness. He was taken at last to a lunatic asylum, where he underwent the severest treatment; this he gladly endured in penance for his sins. He spent two or three months thus confined as a madman. John of Avila, finding him one day reduced to the utmost weakness, advised him to desist from this strange method of penance. John instantly obeyed, and the keepers were surprised to see the sudden change which had come over their patient. He was now allowed to tend and serve the other sufferers, but shortly after he left the asylum.

At the shrine of Our Lady of Guadaloup, whither he went on a pilgrimage, he was favoured with a vision. As he was kneeling before the miraculous image of Our Lady, pondering on what he could do for the relief of the poor and suffering, Mary held out her Infant to him, and gave him garments wherewith to clothe her divine Child. By this vision, John understood that he was to assist the poor of Christ, and in thus exercising charity towards them, he was likewise doing it to Mary's Son. John then returned to Granada, where he knew his cross awaited him. As a means of subsistence, it was his custom to gather faggots of wood, and to sell them in the public squares. Thus he earned a little money, which enabled him to buy bread; but far the greater part he distributed in alms. At this time John was poor and homeless, as poor indeed as any of those on whom he bestowed these alms. A noble lady, named Eleanor of Guivara, was one of the first to appreciate the virtues of the Saint, and she frequently invited him to her house, proud of the honour of receiving him. Towards her John ever entertained the truest affection, and he always called her his "own sister." It was his custom to retire to this lady's oratory to pray. Her daughters, curious to know how he passed the nights there, peeped through the chinks of the door to watch him. There they saw him kneeling through the long hours, rapt in contemplation, his face radiant with a heavenly light.

CHAPTER III.

"The world's a room of sickness, where each heart
  Knows its own anguish and unrest;
The truest wisdom there, and noblest art,
  Is his who skills of comfort best;
Whom by the softest step and gentlest tone
  Enfeebled spirits own,
And love to raise the languid eye,
  When, like an angel's wing, they feel him
    fleeting by."   KEBLE.

JOHN was kneeling one evening before a venerated representation of the crucifixion, with Mary and S. John standing beneath the cross. Suddenly his soul was flooded with heavenly joy, and our Lady and S. John, inclining towards him, placed on his head a thorny crown, while our Lady said to him: "It is through the sufferings caused by these thorns that my Son wills that you should acquire great merit." Then this chivalrous soul replied: "Thorns and suffering, coming from thy sweet hands, O Lady, will be to me as roses." John had an inward conviction that his prayer was heard, and that he was now about to undertake the work for which he had so ardently yearned. Leaving the church, he saw, in one of the adjoining streets, a house on which was the following placard, "House to be let for the poor." Struck by this, John entered, and finding it suitable for his purpose, he resolved at once to rent it. Full of confidence in God, he immediately applied to some devout persons in order to obtain the money he required. This was generously given to him, and with further help he was enabled to set up forty-six beds in the house. It is true they were only composed of rush-mats, with a pillow and two blankets, and over each the Saint hung a wooden cross. When all was ready, he went about the streets seeking the homeless sick and the lame. Thus, in the year 1540, was founded in Granada the first hospital of S. John of God. This charitable undertaking was looked upon as unwise and imprudent. Where indeed was this one poor man to find means to provide for so many invalids? But John cast all his care upon God, knowing that He would not be wanting to him. His trust was rewarded, for by degrees help flowed in from many charitable persons. John's first care was for the souls of the patients, and he urged them to go to confession as soon as they entered the hospital.

Every evening at nine o'clock the indefatigable servant of the poor went out, with a basket on his back, and two copper pots at his sides. He passed through the principal thoroughfares of the city, crying out, "Who wills to do himself good? For the love of God do good to yourselves, my dear brethren." His naturally sweet voice, breaking the stillness with this unheard-of call of charity, roused many to listen, and abundant alms in food or money was bestowed on him. Nothing kept the Saint from his nightly round, returning home about eleven. He then made his last visit to the sick, to see if they had all that was needful. After this he made up his accounts, washed the dishes, and prepared food for the next day. Thus he passed a great part of the night; then he threw himself on his knees, and prayed till darkness fled. One hour was all he allowed himself for sleep. Early in the morning it was his custom to enter the different rooms, and awake the sleepers by saying, " Return thanks to God, my brethren, for this is how the little birds begin the day." After prayer, made in common, the Saint visited each patient in turn, dressing wounds, and ministering to the wants of all. Then, after the sick had breakfasted, he set all things in order; he made the beds, swept and cleaned the rooms. The perfect arrangement and scrupulous cleanliness called forth the highest praise from those who visited the hospital. It was a matter of surprise to all to see the amount of work which the Saint was able to get through without any assistance. His labours for the sick were so dear to God that He often sent the Archangel Raphael to assist him.

On one occasion John was obliged to go a greater distance than usual to fetch the necessary supply of water. He had, in consequence, lost a great part of the morning. On his return he found all his work had been done during his absence, and the sick carefully attended to. His astonishment was great when, on inquiring who had taken his place, every one replied that no one had done so, but that he himself had been seen going about his work as usual. Then said the Saint, "God must indeed love His poor, since He sends His Angels to serve them."

On a certain dark, rainy night, as John was returning from his alms-begging, he heard a poor man calling to him for help. He at once hastened to the sufferer, who was a cripple. The Saint's face was lighted up with heavenly radiance, and the poor man knew then it was John of God. Notwithstanding that he was already heavily laden, the Saint took him on his shoulders, but being overcome with the additional burden, he fell. Then there appeared a person of unspeakable beauty, who lifted the cripple again on John's shoulders. The stranger held out his hand to the Saint, and offered to assist him on his way, saying, " God has sent me to you, Brother John, to help you in your charitable act ; know that He has commanded me to keep an account of all you do for love of Him." " My help always comes from God," answered the Saint; "but tell me, brother, your name." He was wonderstruck when he learnt that the stranger was the Archangel Raphael, to whom God had confided the care of his person. A few days after this event, as John was distributing bread among the sick, he found there was not sufficient for all. Then there appeared the same angelic spirit, dressed exactly like the Saint, holding in his hand a basket of loaves. John instantly recognized the heavenly visitor, who, whispering to him, said, "Brother, we are members of the same order; for men wearing a coarse habit may yet be equal to the Angels. Take this bread, which comes from heaven, to feed your poor sick." Saying this, the Archangel vanished.

On another occasion, one Christmas Eve, John went out to seek for wood on the mountain. Night stole silently on, and the Saint found himself in complete darkness. No moon shone out with welcome light, and the sky was darkened with a coming storm. All in the hospital were greatly concerned for their master's safety, and eagerly inquired which road he had taken. Presently they saw in the distance two lights approaching, but what surprised them the most was that they did not flicker in the boisterous wind. Nearer and nearer the lights approached, till at last, to the joy of all, they beheld John of God, bearing his fagots of wood, walking between the mysterious torches, which only vanished as the Saint reached the threshold of his dwelling.

A still greater favour was vouchsafed to this humble servant of the poor. One night he found a man in the street who seemed to be dying. The Saint at once carried him to the hospital, and there laid him on a bed. As was his custom, he began by washing the dying man's feet. He stooped to kiss them, but what was his astonishment, when he beheld each foot was pierced, and from the wounds there streamed rays of light. Filled with awe, he raised his eyes to the face of Him who lay there, and at once he recognized Christ Crucified, who said to him, "To Me, John, thou doest all thou doest to the poor. I stretch forth My hand for the alms thou givest; thou clothest Me in the person of the poor; Mine are the feet thou dost wash." Then Jesus vanished from before John's ravished gaze. At the moment of His disappearance the room was filled with so bright a light that the terrified sick cried out "Fire! fire!" With gentle words John assured them there was no cause for alarm, and that the light was already extinguished. From that hour the fire of charity burned with increasing vehemence in the heart of the Saint, and he felt no toil or labour was too great for him when it concerned the sick, in whose person he ever after beheld the image of Christ Crucified.

CHAPTER IV.

*" Of body and of soul alike
Thou art physician wise,
And full of joy as if thou wert
Raphael in mortal guise."* FABER.

"DESPISE not thy own flesh," says Isaias: thereby signifying that we should treat our fellow-creatures in the same tender manner as we treat ourselves. All men are one flesh in Christ; so that in despising the poor or sinful, we are in reality despising our own flesh, and reproaching our Maker.

Few Saints have excelled or equalled John of God in his universal charity; for it was by no means confined to the sick in his own hospital. Suffering, or need of any kind in others, filled him with compassion. No one in distress was ever sent away, by him, unrelieved, or at least without some consolation. He secretly sent food and money to indigent widows, and to those, who, from shame, hid their poverty. He was especially vigilant in providing dowers for young girls, who, through poverty, were exposed to the danger of losing their innocence. Nor was he less solicitous for those who had bound themselves to God by a vow of chastity. From rich ladies he begged alms for their support. But lest these virgins should live in idleness, he opened to them the way to gain an honest livelihood. He obliged them to make their own clothes; and for this he begged silk, wool, and flax, which had to be spun, or prepared, before it was fit for use; with these materials they made their own garments. Even the Moorish families, who dwelt in their own quarter of the city, in a disreputable manner, and in the most squalid poverty, were not neglected by the Saint, and his charity to them was rewarded by numerous conversions to Christianity. With all the love of the "Good Shepherd," John did not content himself with seeking out those who were labouring under merely physical infirmities. He knew that Christ, in His mercy, had stooped to raise the fallen, that He had allured Magdalene from a life of sin, and the Saint did not shrink from planting his feet in the footsteps of his dear Lord. But truly it is only one with a heart all on fire, such as was John of God's, who could devote himself with such wonderful perseverance to the conversion of women bound in the shameful fetters of sin. For these unfortunate ones he felt a special compassion; his work among them was often attended with the utmost humiliation, and with the most repulsive ingratitude. Friday was the day chosen by the Saint for his mission of Christ-like charity to their abodes of infamy. As he entered, if he saw one who appeared more shameless than the rest, to her he addressed himself; then, drawing forth his crucifix, and kneeling down, he confessed aloud his own sins, imploring God's pardon with such deep contrition and with so many tears that often the poor abandoned one was so moved that she caught something of the Saint's spirit of compunction, and began to hate her own sinful life. Then John would read to her the account of the Passion in S. John's Gospel, and this he did with such tenderness and unction that it was a depraved heart indeed which was not softened by it.

When some impression was made on the poor sinner's heart, he tenderly called her his dear sister, and urged her to begin at once a new and better life, promising to her fidelity the protection of the everlasting arms, with the assurance of the reward of heaven if she would but lead a life of chastity. The heroic patience of the Saint was not unfrequently immediately rewarded, and the penitent would beg of him to let her follow him at once to serve the sick in his hospital. Many were actually admitted, and to them the Saint confided the care of those who were suffering from the most repulsive diseases. Some of these penitents yearned for a life of perpetual penance, and became very fervent Religious.

As to those who were desirous of quitting sin, but who had not the courage to leave the world, he did his best to promote their marriage by giving them good dowers. In this work the Saint had a generous helper in one named John Fernandez. At his house was prepared the marriage feast, and he himself always presided as host. On one occasion sixteen of these converted women were married on one day. John of God assured Fernandez that his charity would receive its recompense even in this world; and so it was, for the charitable man afterwards made known many occasions on which God had displayed His favourable protection in a miraculous manner.

It is impossible to describe all the obstacles and difficulties which John had to surmount in his apostolate among sinful women; but nothing could exceed the patience and zeal which he exercised in his efforts to reclaim the fallen. Whenever he succeeded in alluring a repentant soul from the bondage of an impure life, her companions would assail him with all manner of reproaches, even accusing him in the most insulting way of evil designs. To all these abominable calumnies the Saint never responded by word or sign, nor would he let any one interfere on his behalf. Sometimes the most wicked ones would make pretence of hearkening to his exhortations, and appear desirous of changing their ways, thus making an abuse of the Saint's charity. On one occasion four of these women, full of hypocrisy, made profession of repentance, and pretended to John that they were resolved to quit their sinful life, but they declared it to be necessary for them to go first to Toledo, their home, where they had business to transact before they could renounce the world. From Granada to Toledo the distance is two hundred miles, a long journey to undertake in those days; but John of God would gladly have gone to the end of the world if by so doing he could save a soul. He therefore agreed to accompany the supposed penitents. To spare them fatigue he mounted them on four mules, and, with one of his disciples, Simon of Avila, he accompanied them on foot. The insulting remarks passed on the strange cortége made no impression on the Saint, who took delight in humiliation and contempt. His companion, however, whose self-abnegation was not so perfect, thought that they had better refrain from undertaking so long and disagreeable a journey. This opinion seemed well founded when, as they reached a certain stage, one of the women managed to elude the vigilance of her conductors, and disappeared. Simon suspected they had been duped, and gave way to his feelings of disgust. On their arrival in Toledo two others likewise escaped; then Simon, full of indignation at such treachery, reproached his master in bitter terms. But the Saint in his gentle way replied, " Suppose, brother, that in carrying four baskets of fish to Granada the contents of three of them were spoiled on the road, so that you were obliged to throw the baskets away, would you for this reason cast aside the remaining one? Do you not think you would value it the more, and be thankful that you had not lost all?" Perhaps the Saint's meekness and humility made an impression on the sinner who remained, for she promised to keep faithful to her word, and returned at once with John and Simon to Granada. In time she married, and after her husband's death she led a life of extraordinary sanctity.

Such universal charity gained the admiration of every one. The rich and noble considered it an honour to entertain the servant of the poor, and they were ever ready to respond to his constant call of charity.

One day the Saint went to the Bishop of Tuy, then president of the court of judicature in Granada, to solicit alms. He made a most favourable impression on the prelate, who bade him ever keep the name of John of God. Remarking that the Saint wore no garment like a habit, he ordered a piece of coarse cloth to be brought to him, and prescribed the form of the dress which he desired John henceforth to wear. "For virtue," said the bishop, "does not consist in tattered garments, but in the exercise of good deeds." From this time John of God never wore any dress but the one appointed by the holy prelate. It became the habit of the Brothers of his Order, although at the time of his visit to the bishop John had no intention of founding one. This event, however, was the first faint glimmering of that institute of charity which was to perpetuate the compassionate love of S. John of God for the poor and suffering.

CHAPTER V.

*"Then men would come with thee to dwell
 Beneath the shade of love's own roof:
Thy life in them was woven well,
 And shadowed forth the Christ by proof."*

NOTHING in the early manhood of Anthony Martin, or of Peter Velasco, foreshadowed their future holiness. They were men who seemed little likely to become the disciples of S. John of God, and so to bear meekly the sweet yoke of Christ. They were deadly enemies, for Martin's brother had been slain by Velasco. Martin determined to revenge the crime by the death of him who had been its perpetrator. He came, therefore, to Granada to demand justice at the hands of the law. He never rested till his foe was imprisoned, and he declared that nothing would content him but to see Velasco hanging on the gallows. He was, however, obliged to wait until the affair could be judicially inquired into, for in those days trial for capital punishment was conducted very slowly. In the meanwhile Martin led a most dissolute life, his immorality being a public cause of scandal. His vanity was displayed in the magnificence of his velvet mantle, his jewel-hilted sword, and plumed cap, the love of fine attire being deeply rooted in his heart. There was, however, one redeeming point in his character, compassion for the poor, and to John of God he never refused to give an alms. Thus the sinner was counted by the Saint as one of his friends and benefactors, for John knew that one day this charity would meet with its certain reward.

Those who lead a sumptuous life are sure to collect around them a number of sycophants, like flies caught by the smell of the honey jar. Martin was not without such followers, and as the law-suit against Velasco was drawing to a close, and the long-desired sentence about to be pronounced on the delinquent, some of the better-intentioned among them, in concert with the friends of Velasco, tried every means to soften Martin's anger against his foe. But neither the rank of the intercessors nor the earnestness of their appeal made the slightest impression on the enraged man. He persisted in his thirst for vengeance, and would listen neither to the voice of religion nor of reason.

There was one person, however, who did not despair of a change being wrought in Martin's heart, and this was John of God. Doubtless he had wrestled long in prayer for Anthony's soul before he determined to see if he could not induce him to be reconciled with his adversary. To this end the Saint set out to call on Martin. They met in one of the public squares, and there John threw himself on his knees, and holding up the crucifix, said, "Brother, in order to gain God's pardon, thou must, at my prayer, consent to forgive thy enemy. Remember in how many ways thou hast thyself offended God, and so learn mercy for him who has offended thee much less. God will show no mercy to him who has been hard on his brother. If thy enemy has shed thy brother's blood, have not we already caused Christ's precious Blood to flow in a still more copious stream? Hearken, then, to the voice of that Divine Blood which implores thy pardon, rather than to that of thy brother which cries to thee for vengeance."

While John was making this appeal the angels were clustering round the sinner's heart, and showering on it the dew of heaven, and as the divine drops fell one by one on the arid ground, gradually it was softened, and mercy, like a lily, sprang up in that heart which had hitherto borne only the briers of hatred and revenge. We can easily conceive the gladness which filled the Saint's heart as the following words fell upon his ear: "John of God, at your prayer I not only pardon him to whom I have sworn an eternal hatred, but I humbly offer myself to be your disciple. You have saved Velasco's life; help me now to save my soul. If I lead you to the dungeon where he lies captive, that you may set him free, will you not in return let me follow you to your hospital, that I may there consecrate my life and all I possess to God and to the service of His poor? Your words have kindled this desire in my heart; your example will aid me in fulfilling it."

Without delay John of God and

Anthony Martin proceeded to the prison. Peace was made between the foes, and Velasco set at liberty. Filled with admiration and gratitude, he likewise pleaded to be allowed to follow the Saint in serving Christ's poor. Thus from that day these two lived as brothers, wearing the same habit as S. John, and, like him, wholly devoted to the service of the sick.

Anthony Martin reached an eminent degree of sanctity. Among all John's disciples he was considered to be the most devoted and the most exemplary follower of his master. After the death of S. John he was elected superior in his place.

As to Velasco, it suffices to say that grace made such a deep impression on his heart that he devoted himself to his work with the perfect dispositions of a true penitent, the perfume of his humility betraying itself, violet-like, from beneath the broad leaves of his wonderful penance.

By the side of these two strange vocations there is another likewise worthy of mention, that of Simon of Avila. Although a devout man, he was incredulous as to the sanctity of John of God; he believed him to be an impostor; and with the intention, as he thought, of unmasking the Saint's hypocrisy, he was ever on the alert to detect some flaw in John's conduct.

One evening Simon watched the Saint enter a certain house where dwelt a widow with her three little children. To them John was carrying their evening meal. This greatly excited Simon's suspicion. "Now," thought he, "I have surely found him out, for this is no hour for calls of charity." Stealthily following him, therefore, he glanced through a chink in the doorway, to see what was passing within. To his surprise, instead of beholding the spectacle which his evil suspicions had led him to expect, his eyes fell on a blank wall, on which was inscribed the long list of all his past sins, and a flaming sword appeared ready to fall upon his head. At this terrible vision Simon swooned with fear. The noise of his fall brought S. John to the spot, who, finding him almost inanimate, invoked the name of Jesus, and, making the sign of the cross on Simon's breast, recalled him to consciousness. That same night Simon of Avila bent his steps to S. John's hospital, and casting himself on his knees, confessed to the Saint the abominable suspicions which he had entertained against him. Neither did he hide the wicked curiosity which had led him to play the spy that night, nor the dreadful vision which had been its punishment. He implored of John not only to pardon him, but also to admit him among the number of his disciples. The Saint recognized the marks of a true vocation, and he gladly received him as a brother. With the utmost abnegation and tender sympathy Simon devoted himself to the service of the poor. He was a pattern of all virtues during the thirteen years he laboured on earth before he passed to peace eternal.

John was always ready to receive those in whom he saw marks of a real vocation. He was gifted, Gouvea tells us, with a supernatural light which enabled him clearly to discern those whom God called to be his disciples. No worldly consideration or human interest ever prompted him to accept any one if he did not think their vocation came from heaven. A proof of this is shown in the following occurrence.

A rich young nobleman, by name Ferdinand Nunnes, was enamoured of a certain damsel. To attract the maiden's attention, the young cavalier would often pass beneath her window on a prancing steed. Worldly-minded as he was, and with thoughts bent on matrimony, his heart was at times tormented with a feeling that he was called to renounce his golden dreams of love. A void was left in his heart which none but God could fill. Having heard of John's charity, he resolved to give him a large sum of money, that by so doing he might draw down on his own soul grace to know in what way it was God's pleasure that he should walk. As John was personally unknown to him, Ferdinand resolved to put his charity to the test. One evening, on meeting the Saint at the gates of the city, the young man drew him aside, telling him that he belonged to an illustrious house, that he was in immediate want of two hundred ducats, but that he knew not where to turn for this sum. "If it be in your power," he said, "to give me this money, do so. for the love of God; but if you have it not, help me by your prayers, lest I take some desperate step." Such an appeal was not likely to be rejected by the Saint. He bade the young man to meet him the next night at the same hour and place, promising that in the meanwhile, he would endeavour to collect the money.

A king trusting to his royal treasures could not have felt more certain of being able to procure the required amount than was John of God, whose only treasure lay in his trust in God's goodness. His hope was rewarded, and from the charity of others John was able to draw the money. At the trysting-place the Saint and the cavalier met at the appointed hour. "Thank God," said the former, "I have all you want; here it is in my wallet." At these words Ferdinand was wonderstruck at the charity of the Saint to a stranger. Then tenderly embracing John, he told him to keep the money he had so generously collected, and further begged of his acceptance of two hundred more ducats for his poor. He avowed the object of his ruse, and begged the Saint's prayers to know what God required of him.

Shortly after this, as he was passing beneath the balcony of his beloved, Ferdinand's horse suddenly stopped, and neither spur nor whip would induce it to move one step. Bending forward, the young man beheld a yawning gulf, and in his terror he raised his eyes to heaven. Then the clouds seemed to roll backward, and a flood of light streamed down. By this Ferdinand understood that if he entered the marriage state it would be the cause of his ruin, but renouncing worldly delights, heaven would be given to him in exchange. This manifestation he felt to be the fruit of S. John's prayer, and he hastened to make known to him what had happened. But the Saint, who no doubt knew by a secret inspiration that Ferdinand was not called to be his disciple, sent him to seek advice from John of Avila. This one counselled him to study for the priesthood. After distributing his princely fortune among God's poor, Ferdinand in time was ordained. He led a life of such wonderful holiness that some have judged him worthy of being canonized.

CHAPTER VI.

"True friendship is the hallowed tie
  That binds two souls in one;
Their hopes and fears all mingled lie
  As threads together spun.
Sweet gift to man, divinely given,
As foretaste of the love of heaven."

AS time went on, John had many helpers in his work; he therefore had more leisure for collecting alms. He never left the hospital without having visited each one of his sick, for they ever remained the dearest objects of his care. At ten in the morning he started on his rounds, and returned home about eleven at night. His begging was not confined to Granada; he solicited alms likewise in Castile, and in many places in Andalusia. In these towns he only begged from the rich, while in Granada he received alike from rich and poor. A beautiful incident is recorded of the charity of a poor woman, which made a great sensation in the city.

There dwelt in Granada a widow, who, although in poverty, would never let S. John pass her door without giving him something. On one occasion she had absolutely nothing to offer him but a handful of salt. The Saint accepted it, blessing her for her gift. The poor woman was soon to learn how acceptable it had been to God, and how well He rewards those who are good to His poor. Unknown to the widow, her soldier son had obtained leave of absence. On his way home, being without any money, he was obliged to beg for his daily food. On his arrival he did not fail to recount to his mother all that had happened to him, and the hardships he had met with. Nevertheless he declared that he had never failed but once in getting his daily meal, and on that day he had only received a handful of salt. This reminded the widow of a similar alms she had given a few days previously to John of God. On questioning her son, she found he had been given the salt on the very day she had given her handful to the Saint. Her heart sang for joy as she discovered that the alms which her son had received each day corresponded precisely in substance and quantity with what she had deprived herself of in order to bestow it on the poor. When this wonderful story became known, the citizens of Granada recognized the truth of their dear Saint's call of charity, when he cried, "Do good to yourselves in giving to the poor."

It is impossible to mention the names of all those who were honoured by the friendship of the Saint. The Duke and Duchess of Sessa were among the most illustrious. They took the liveliest interest in the hospital and its inmates. On the great festivals it was the duke's custom to send to S. John a quantity of clothing and shoes for the poor in addition to his usual gifts. This saintly couple were childless, but John of God predicted to the duchess that she would become the mother of a child of blessing, which prediction was fulfilled.

A brave Spanish knight, Laso de la Vega, was another friend very dear to John's heart; their affection was mutual. Laso was one of the very few to whom the Saint made known his troubles, for money matters often pressed very heavily on his heart. He finishes a letter to Laso by saying, "I put all my trust in Christ to free me from my debts, for they are a heavy burden to my spirit; but I am not afraid, my well-beloved brother, to make known to you my troubles, for I know well that your heart sympathises in all that concerns me." Laso was anxious about the future of his sons. The Saint predicted to him that one would become a priest, and the other would marry.

The wife of Don Garcia de Pisa, Anna Ossorio, a lady as virtuous as she was noble, was the Saint's most generous helper, and the most zealous in forwarding all his works of charity. She held him in the highest veneration, and she never felt more honoured than when she received his visits, and he consented to sit at her table. Donna Anna and the Saint were ever knit in the holy bonds of friendship, and it was at her house that the Saint breathed his last.

Mention has been already made of John Fernandez and of Donna Eleanor Guevara, who were likewise honoured with the Saint's affection.

Like most of God's servants, John was not without his enemies, but by his patience and gentle forbearance many of these became in time his friends and benefactors.

On one of the many occasions when the Saint was in great need of money, he determined to borrow some from a merchant named Piola. As the Saint called to make his request, Piola and his wife were at table, but so urgent was the case that John persisted in seeing them.

"Brother," said he to the merchant, "my poor are in great want; I implore of you, in God's name, to lend me thirty pieces of gold."

Neither the merchant nor his wife felt inclined to accede to the Saint's request. The latter indeed was so indignant that without further ado she rose from table and left the room. When his wife was out of hearing, Piola asked John what guarantee he could offer for the return of the money. "This," replied the Saint, handing him a picture of the Child Jesus, which he always carried about with him. The merchant rather incredulously looked at the print, when lo! he beheld the figure of the Divine Infant was bright with an unearthly radiance. Then a change came over the heart of the hard, money-loving man. Hitherto he had held the Saint in no great estimation, and had often criticised his works of charity. Now he was filled with admiration, and he eagerly gave to S. John the required sum of money.

Years afterwards, on the death of his wife, Piola became one of John's most devoted followers, and after the Saint's death he was appointed to collect the daily alms.

John of God had his personal enemies and the enemies to his work. Many of the vulgar-minded still looked upon John as a madman; his charity was, to their narrow minds, nothing better than a mania. There were others who absolutely refused to believe in his sanctity, and considered him a hypocrite. Even among the poor there were some who thought themselves creditors to his charity, and whose demands for money it was impossible to satisfy. One man had the insolence to strike the Saint, abusing him without measure, and this because he was given an alms which he considered paltry. One of the women whom the Saint had delivered from the bondage of a sinful life, made such an abuse of his kindness that she demanded from him all she wanted, not as a charity, but as her due. Once she came to John, and insisted on his giving her some linen. Not having any just then, he bade her come again the next day. Offended by the refusal, she poured out a torrent of vilest language, calling the Saint by every foul name. John waited quietly till the storm was past, then said he gently, "Sooner or later I must pardon you; I prefer doing so at once."

There were others who went so far as to criticize the Saint's management of the hospital, accusing him of making a bad use of the money given to him in alms. In fact, there was not one of his good works which escaped the vile abuse of the slanderer's tongue.

CHAPTER VII.

> "In vain the waves in crested line
> Assail love's bark in hearts like thine,
> Though all around expire;
> For naught can wreck the craft divine,
> Nor death, nor flame of fire."

AS preparations for a banquet were one day being made in the royal hospital of Granada, a fire broke out from the under storey of the building. So rapid was the spread of the flames that it was soon feared that this monument of royal munificence would be completely destroyed. The sound of the tocsin brought multitudes to the spot, and although the hospital was situated in a spacious plain, there was scarcely room enough to contain the vast crowd which soon was gathered around its walls. The fire raged with wild fury, and through the thick veil of smoke a huge mass of flame leaped up in savage glare. Consternation filled every breast, and fear was depicted on the sea of the upturned faces of the spectators. Some advised sending for the artillery to demolish the already burning wing, in the hope of thus saving the other portions of the building. But there were the poor inmates to be thought of; were they to be sacrificed for the sake of the edifice? Many of these unfortunate beings were seen at the windows, supplicating by their gestures for help. Amidst that vast throng there was not one who had the courage to risk his life in the hope of being able to save others from a dreadful death. Suddenly a murmur was heard, and a thrill of admiration moved the one heart of the mighty concourse, as a man clad in a dark garment was seen hastening towards the burning building. The figure, which was instantly recognized to be that of John of God, passed beneath the portal, from which issued a torrent of black smoke. For a few minutes there was a breathless silence; but a burst of applause broke as if from one voice as the Saint was seen opening the doors, and leading the patients to the various exits. As the peril became greater, and flight more impossible, the brave-hearted man went through the different wards, and bearing the sufferers in turn upon his shoulders, he aided them to escape by the windows. Those who were helpless he secured to mattresses, and gently let them down to the ground. Thus every inmate of the hospital was saved through the heroism of the Saint.

Not yet satisfied, John looked about to see if he could not snatch something from the greedy flames. Mattresses, bed-clothes, linen, anything he could lay his hands on, he eagerly threw from the windows. At last his generous work seemed ended, crowned indeed with unhoped-for success. The flames appeared to have let him have his way in their very midst; but surely now he must make his escape from the sea of fire which was surging all around. Many hundred eyes were bent on his every movement, when suddenly he disappeared from their sight.

From the thinly constructed roof the fire was now spreading, and John had conceived the perilous design of cutting it open, so as to let the flames escape more surely. As the Saint re-appeared on the roof with a hatchet in his hand, the spectators shuddered as they thought of the danger to which he was exposing himself. There stood the heroic man in the midst of the cloud of fire, hewing with all his might at the quickly yielding wood. Then he was seen no more, and a cry of anguish burst from the breathless throng; all felt sure that the Saint had fallen a victim to his daring heroism. But the mighty arm of God was still shielding His servant, and to the delight of all the beholders he was again seen on the opposite side of the building. He succeeded in making a separation sufficient to arrest the progress of the fire, and thus one wing of the edifice was saved. At the end of half an hour John left his work, and then came forth, to the marvel of all, calm and self-possessed, but what was more wonderful, unhurt. His eye-lashes alone were completely burnt away, thus bearing witness to his miraculous preservation. His heart, aflame with the love of God, had led him to throw himself fearlessly amid the fire, and God had rewarded his charity.

After this event alms flowed more

abundantly into the hands of the Saint, and as the number of his sick had greatly increased he now resolved to found a more commodious hospital. The citizens of Granada gladly assisted him, and an old convent was bought for the purpose.

John was now able to receive a larger number of patients, but as they increased his expenses were likewise greater. His friends advised him to go to Valladolid, where the court then resided. Thither he accordingly went, and presented himself to the Infant Don Philip and his sisters. He was received by them in the most courteous manner, and they bestowed on him large sums of money. Following their princely example, many ladies generously sold their jewels in order to give their value to the Saint.

During his sojourn in Valladolid John was the guest of Donna Maria de Mendoza, mother of the pious Duchess of

Sessa. She led a life of great holiness, and was favoured of God with uncommon graces. It was her joy to entertain him who bore the name of "the Saint of Granada."

John's reputation, however, was not confined to the great and wealthy. The sweet odour of his charity spread itself like wreaths of incense around, and the poor were quickly drawn to one who was the acknowledged friend of the needy. Nor did the Saint close his ears to their pleading because they were strangers to him, and he had only come to their city to collect alms for his own poor in Granada. His love for his neighbour was Christ-like; how then could he see his brother in need and not show mercy to him? Freely did he bestow money or assistance on all who sought his aid; he visited the sick, consoled the sorrowful, and reclaimed the sinful. In this manner the money he had collected soon vanished, and he was rebuked by many for thus spending the alms which had been given to him for his own suffering ones. "What matters it," replied the Saint, "if I relieve the poor here or in Granada? My alms are always given to God, and is He not everywhere and in the person of all the needy?"

For nine months John tarried in Valladolid. It was in the summer-time that he took his departure. His was a painful home-journey, made beneath the ardent sun, and on the dusty Spanish roads. His bare head and feet were blistered, and he suffered intensely from the heat. The fatigue he underwent brought on great exhaustion, which undermined the Saint's naturally robust constitution, and in the end led to the illness which caused his death.

John's return was the cause of joy throughout Granada. The poor flocked to welcome him, and his sick rejoiced with an overwhelming joy to find their master once more among them.

The austerity of John's life, his long journeys at all times and in all weathers, his want of sleep, and his bodily mortifications, had now reduced him to a state of great weakness; but this did not make him change his manner of life. He was as indefatigable as ever in the service of the poor, and while his own strength was wasting away he still thought only of the means by which he could afford relief to his afflicted fellow-creatures. He kept his own sufferings a secret, for he could not bear to think of the sorrow which the knowledge of them would cause to others. He knew well enough that his life was drawing near its close, for S. Raphael had revealed to him the day and hour of his deliverance. In the meanwhile he made regulations for the hospital, inspected his accounts, and silently made ready for his departure from this world.

The immediate cause of the Saint's death-sickness was a chill brought on by an excess of fatigue in saving wood for the poor in the overflow of the Xenil. Heedless of his own exhaustion, he plunged into the waters to save the life of a boy who had ventured too far, and was being carried along by the rushing stream. The Saint's efforts were, however, unavailing, and, to his great distress, the youth perished.

CHAPTER VIII.

> "As fades the light at close of day,
> So passed thy soul from earth away,
> Rapt in a trance of prayer.
> And at the moment of thy death
> A fragrance, like an Angel's breath,
> Was wafted on the air."

THE shades of night were fading and the day about to break, when the soul of God's servant was to leave its earthly tabernacle, and wing its flight to heaven. Already he could hear the Bridegroom whisper, "Make haste, My love, and come." For now he was confined to his bed of sickness, and it was evident to all that he would not be with them long.

The citizens of Granada, seeing the Saint no longer on his rounds of charity, knew that he must be seriously ill, and great was their sorrow when the news of his increasing illness was spread abroad. They flocked to offer him all that was needful to his comfort, not forgetting to carry him the alms which they had been in the habit of giving him.

As soon as Donna Ossorio heard of her friend's illness she hastened to visit him. She was moved with pity when she found him lying on an old straw mattress laid on the floor, his head supported by a basket which had served him to carry food to his poor, his only covering being an old mantle. She knew how necessary rest was for the sufferer, and she determined to have him removed to her own house, where she could tend him. She proposed to S. John that he should go with her at once, but he begged so earnestly to be allowed to remain to die among his beloved sick that she had not the heart to insist. Hoping that with care the life of the Saint might yet be spared, Donna Ossorio secretly sent a message to the Archbishop, begging of him to use his authority with John, and command him, under obedience, to put no obstacle to the means offered to effect his cure. The prelate did as she asked, and sent word to the Saint that he was to obey Donna Ossorio as he would do himself, and that as he had always preached obedience to others, now he must make an act of self-sacrifice, and do what was asked of him. The holy man gave in at once, and consented to be taken to the house of his friend.

But how was he to be carried away without the knowledge of the sick? When they heard their master was to be taken from them, all those who were able to move came round him. Then followed a piteous scene; some clinging to his garments, others kissing his hands, all weeping bitter tears. The tender heart of the Saint could not resist such touching marks of affection; mingling his tears with theirs, and in a voice broken by sobs, he said, "God knows, brethren, that I would rather die in your midst, but as He ordains otherwise His holy will be done." After blessing each one in turn, he added, "Peace be with you, dear children: and if we never meet again in this world, pray for me." These words excited renewed grief in the hearts of the bystanders, and they became still more vehement in their demonstrations of sorrow. The emotion caused by this scene made the Saint to swoon away. As soon as he recovered he was immediately taken to Donna Ossorio's. Here with gentle hands and loving heart he was carefully tended, and with childlike obedience he took all the remedies which were prescribed for him. Thanks to the care bestowed upon him, he lived on for a few weeks. "Love is strong as death," and of this the Saint gave witness on the last day of his sojourn on earth. It is from Gouvea we learn the following incident.

At this time provisions were very dear in Granada, and a poor weaver, through poverty, was brought to such a miserable frame of mind that he resolved to put an end to his existence. Thus one morning he rose, and securing a rope, he hastened to a wood, there to hang himself.

As John lay sleepless through the night, he passed the hours in prayer for his sick, and in recommending the poor to the care of their heavenly Father. While thus engaged he received a revelation of the state of the weaver's soul, and of his evil determination. When morning dawned, the Saint rose from his bed, and dressing himself quickly, he begged of the attendants to let him pass out. They wondered what it meant, and thinking he was in delirium, they tried to persuade him to return to his bed. The Saint implored to be allowed to have his way, assuring them he had a mission to fulfil which was for God's glory, and he promised to be away no long time. Yielding at last to his entreaties, his attendants opened the doors for him to depart. Swift as the hart the Saint made his way to the wood, where the weaver was already preparing for his work of death; but seeing some one approach, he hid the rope. In the gentlest manner the Saint saluted him, and then revealed to him the sinful state of his soul. His words brought back hope to the sinner's breast, and with tears of gratitude he thanked the Saint for having thus snatched him from the jaws of hell.

Filled with joy at having gained one

more soul to God, and after telling the weaver to apply for assistance from a person he named, John hastened to return home. Great was the anxiety felt on his account, and to Donna Ossorio he was forced to confess what had called him forth that morning.

Then he told his dear benefactress that he had but a few hours to pass on earth. He requested that Anthony Martin should be sent for, and to him John recommended the care of his hospital, the sick, and the suffering poor. Laying aside his usual reserve on the subject of his heavenly favours, the dying Saint revealed to his beloved disciple a vision which had been vouchsafed to him.

The Archbishop had given leave for Mass to be said in the room where he lay, and while making his thanksgiving, after receiving Viaticum, our Lady, with S. Raphael and S. John the Evangelist, appeared to him. He told how the gracious Mother of God had wiped from his forehead the dew of death, and had promised to take his poor under her especial protection. No doubt he made known this revelation to Anthony to comfort him, as he was now to undertake the care of the poor, which S. John was leaving him as a heritage.

As the Saint was unable to receive Holy Communion, he begged that the Blessed Sacrament should be brought into his room, that he might at least adore it for the last time. As soon as the Sacred Host was laid on the altar the Saint desired to be left alone with his God. When all had retired he rose from his bed, and remained kneeling for a considerable time in prayer; then in a loud voice he cried, "Into Thy hands, O Jesus, I commend my spirit." And so saying, he breathed forth his soul to God.

On hearing these words, those who were waiting without gently pushed aside the door; but, seeing John was still kneeling with the crucifix clasped to his breast, they withdrew, for fear of disturbing him. Time sped on, and as no sound was heard they determined to re-enter the room. There they found the Saint still motionless in the same prayerful attitude, and again they hesitated to advance; but on perceiving the room was filled with an exquisite fragrance, they at once recognized the sign by which God was pleased to mark the death of His servant. Drawing near to the kneeling figure, they found indeed that the Angels had borne his blessed soul to heaven.

No change took place in the position of the Saint's body. He looked as if in extasy, his head uplifted, his figure upright, and his hands firmly clasped about the crucifix. On his face there rested no trace of pain; perfect peace and happiness were mirrored in the tranquil beauty and repose of his whole figure. " Precious in the sight of the Lord is the death of His Saints;" and S. John's departure from life had been as calm as the fading of the evening light in a summer sky.

The sacred stillness was broken by the mourning friends of the Saint, who gave free vent to their tears; but their hearts were calm and submissive, for they felt that he whom they loved so well was now surely in the enjoyment of heaven.

As the Saint still continued in the same immoveable posture, fears were entertained of the impossibility of laying him on the bier, so gently and reverently his limbs were straightened, and Donna Ossorio had the blessed body placed on a bed of state, and the room adorned with great magnificence.

His funeral was conducted with extraordinary honour, his sacred remains being deposited in the mortuary chapel of the house of Ossorio in the Church of our Lady of Victories.

The delicious fragrance which had filled the room at the Saint's death did not pass away for nine days; from that time it was perceptible every Saturday at the hour he had expired.

Twenty years after S. John's death, the Archbishop of Granada, being informed that an extraordinary light was constantly seen to issue from the mortuary chapel where he lay, determined to investigate the matter. As soon as the coffin was opened the same sweet odour escaped from the incorrupt body of the Saint. But this was not the only manifest sign of John's sanctity, for a poor cripple was instantly cured of his infirmity on merely drawing near to the lifeless body. The tomb was reopened some years later, and this fragrance was again wafted on the air. The relics of the Saint were then removed to a shrine beneath the altar, but at the oft-repeated prayer of the Brothers of his Order they were finally removed to their church in 1664.

S. John of God died on his fifty-fifth birthday, the 8th of March, 1550, and he was canonized by Pope Alexander VIII. on the 16th of October, 1690.

CHAPTER IX.

*"As springs the herb in sheltered nook,
As willow by the running brook,
    So grew all grace in thee.
As sweetest honey in the mouth,
As breezes from the sunny south,
    So is thy name to me."*

MID a basket of flowers there is always one blossom whose breath is more fragrant than the rest, their sweetness being enhanced by blending with it. So we generally find the hearts of the Saints were redolent of the virtue in which they excelled, and that from it sprang all the nobleness, the power, and the beauty of their lives. The special virtue of founders of religious orders breathes its own perfume on its individual institute, and becomes the characteristic mark of its members.

Thus in the heart of John of God charity was the flower which lent fragrance to all his virtues, the seal which is imprinted on his order, and on the hearts of his followers. His was a mission of charity, and for this he was endowed with a tender, generous, and merciful heart. Few Saints have equalled him in the heroism of his virtue. Charity was the mainspring of all his actions. Firstly, charity towards God, true, deep, and intense, and from this love sprang compassion for his fellow-creatures. In the poor and suffering he venerated Christ crucified, and in the sinful he beheld souls for whom Jesus was yearning. The tenderness with which he devoted himself to the service of the sick was likewise the fruit of his love of God. Charity was to the Saint a spiritual ladder by which he ascended to God, and by which he descended to aid his needy brethren. He fed the hungry, clothed the naked, harboured the harbourless. Decrepit age, vigorous manhood, youth, and helpless infancy, all found a friend and comforter in S. John. No opportunity was neglected by him of doing good to others; never did he turn a deaf ear to the petition of those who asked for charity in God's name, or for love of Him. In the poor he ever recognized the person of our Lord, and thus, friends or enemies, strangers or those known to him, were all treated alike with the same compassionate tenderness.

As charity towards his brethren flowed from the Saint's love of God, so was it the fount of all his other virtues. This love gave birth in his heart to deep gratitude for all that Christ had suffered for him, and this gratitude became deeper as his compunction for sin grew more profound. Thus he yearned to sacrifice himself in full measure, as Christ had sacrificed Himself for men. This explains his wonderful silence and patience in bearing humiliation, injustice, and insult. His one desire was to imitate, as closely as he could, the life of our Blessed Lord, and thus he did his best to follow his divine Model in charity, humility, poverty, and zeal for souls.

From the days of his childhood the Saint was filled with the spirit of prayer. His every breath was a dart of love towards God. Prayer was his shield, his delight, and his refuge. As the hours of day were occupied, the night was set apart by the Saint for his recollections. While praying, a luminous ray was frequently seen to issue from his mouth, an evident sign of the ardour of his prayer, and of its acceptance in the sight of heaven.

The devil, finding that he could not prevent the Saint's constant prayer, tried at least to distract him from it. As S. John was once praying in church, the fiend took the form of a bat, and kept flying round the lamp of the sanctuary, and at length stooped to drink the oil. Seeing this, the Saint rose, and clapping with his hands, endeavoured to frighten it away. Instead of so doing, the evil one said aloud, "So I have at last happily succeeded in distracting thee at thy prayer." Undisturbed by the strange speaker, the Saint replied, "You have gained nothing thereby, for in reparation of the time you have made me lose, I shall doubly prolong my prayer which is so hateful to you."

Saint John's two principal devotions were to the sacred Passion and to our Blessed Lady. To her he turned for help in all his troubles, and wonderful was the protection with which she rewarded his child-like confidence.

Prayer unsustained by mortification is but a feeble thing; it is mortification which gives wings to prayer, and bears it to the throne of God. S. John's life was one of intense self-denial. Constant attendance on the sick is not pleasant to human nature, yet their fretful murmurs and ingratitude are often harder to bear than actual service. What a source of mortification must all this have been to the Saint, who never refused to receive under his care the most forbidding subjects, or those afflicted with the most repulsive diseases.

In order to keep the flesh fully submissive to the spirit, he crucified his appetite and desires in every possible way, allowing to his body only the absolutely necessary. He never took more than one hour's sleep, and this on a mattress laid on the floor, a stone serving for a pillow, and an old mantle for a covering. He ate very sparingly, contenting himself with the commonest sort of food. On fast-days he scarcely tasted anything, and every Friday his food consisted only of bread and water. His disciplines were so dreadful that the blood would stream down his body, and this when he was exhausted by sickness or fatigue. From the day of his vision of the Child Jesus he could never be induced to wear shoes or a covering on his head.

Although the Saint was so hard on himself, he was tenderness itself towards others. In a letter to the Duchess of Sessa he begs of her to take needful care of her body, as it is important to keep it in a good state of health; "but," he added, "it should be treated as a domestic animal which is to render us a useful but laborious service."

Another rill of virtue flowing from

the broad stream of the Saint's charity was self-abnegation. No outrage or insult ever ruffled the peace of his soul. He had sinned, and he took delight in humiliation as a source of reparation for the past. His desire to resemble Christ in all things made him thirst for contempt and infamy; he prized these things above gold, and the derision of the world was dearer to him than all her honours.

Humility was so deeply rooted in the heart of the Saint that no shaft was ever able to wound it. When men were drawn to love him for his spotless life, and for the sweet tenderness of his soul so full of human sympathy, and when praise was showered on his name and works, he only took occasion therefrom to humble himself the more deeply, and to acknowledge that God had indeed chosen a most worthless instrument to show forth the greatness of His love and power.

God rewarded the fidelity of His servant by bestowing on him many gracious tokens of love. He endowed him with the gift of prophecy and spiritual discernment, unveiled to him the secrets of souls, and frequently made known to him the coming death of those under his care. Angelic spirits were his helpmates, and often did some heavenly vision hold his soul rapt in long and silent contemplation.

Of the beautiful picture of the life of S. John of God this is but a roughly-drawn sketch. The graceful figure of the Saint should stand out in its own striking beauty, glowing with the rich colours of charity, fitly set off by the dark shadings of abnegation and penance.

It is well for us in these our self-indulgent days to let one's eyes rest on this grand old Spanish picture. In taking it for our model we may try to catch a something of its glory, and putting forth all our skill, endeavour to produce in our own lives some faint copy of its undying loveliness, a beauty that can never fade away.

Richardson and Son, Printers, Derby.

RICHARDSON AND SON'S PUBLICATIONS.
23, King Edward Street, City, London, E.C.; and Derby.

LIFE OF ST. JOHN BAPTIST DE ROSSI,
Translated from the Italian, by LADY HERBERT. With an Introduction on **Ecclesiastical Training and the Sacerdotal Life,** by the BISHOP OF SALFORD. Demy 8vo, with PORTRAIT OF THE SAINT, superfine cloth, lettered in gold, price 6s.

THE LIFE OF DOM BARTHOLOMEW OF THE MARTYRS, Religious of the Order
of St. Dominic, Archbishop of Braga in Portugal, translated from his Biographies. By LADY HERBERT. Demy 8vo, extra cloth, price 12s. 6d.

"Lady Herbert's large Life of this wonderful servant of God—Dom Bartholomew of the Martyrs—has become a standard work on the ecclesiastical spirit, and a perfect treasury for Priests and Bishops."—FROM THE BISHOP OF SALFORD.

Heaven Opened; or, our Home in Heaven,
and the Way Thither. A Manual of Guidance for Devout Souls. By Rev. Father Collins. Post 8vo, handsomely bound, price 5s.

The Cistercian Fathers, or Lives and
Legends of certain Saints and Blessed of the Order of Citeaux, translated by the Rev. HENRY COLLINS. With a Preface by the Rev. W. R. Brownlow, M.A., one of the Editors of "Roma Sotterranea." First Series, 4s.

The Cistercian Fathers. (Second Series.) Translated by Rev. Henry Collins. Price 4s. 6d.

Mediæval Legends, from Cesar of Heisterbach.
Translated by Henry Collins. With a Steel Engraving of the Abbey of Mount St. Bernard, Leicestershire. Foolscap 8vo, cloth extra, price 3s.

The Virgin Mary According to the Gospel.
By Nicolas. Translated by the Vicomtesse de L. S. J., and Sister M. Christopher, O.S.F. Edited by the Rev. H. Collins. Post 8vo, superfine cloth, price 6s. 6d.

RICHARDSON AND SON'S PUBLICATIONS.
23, King Edward Street, City, London, E.C.; and Derby.

MINIATURE WORKS OF DEVOTIONAL AND PRACTICAL PIETY.

Demy 18mo, handsomely bound in cloth, price 6d. each.

Meditations on the Seven Gifts of the Holy GHOST. By Father Pergmayer, S.J.

Communion Prayers for Every Day of the WEEK. By Canon A. C. Arvisenet.

Heavenward. From "Heaven Opened." By Rev. Father Collins.

Month of Jesus Christ. By S. Bonaventure.

Comfort for Mourners. By S. Francis of Sales. From his Letters. Translated by E. M. B.

Stations of the Passion as made in Jerusalem, and Select Devotions on the Passion, from the Prayers of S. Gertrude, O.S.B. Translated by Rev. H. Collins.

Holy Will of God: a Short Rule of Perfection. By Father Benedict Canfield. Translated by Father Collins.

The Our Father: Meditations on the Lord's Prayer. By St. Teresa. Translated by E. M. B.

The Quiet of the Soul. By Father John de Bovilla. To which is added, **Cure for Scruples.** By Dom Schram, O.S.B. Edited by the Rev. H. Collins.

Little Manual of Direction, for Priests, Religious Superiors, Novice-Masters and Mistresses, &c. By Dom Schram, O.S.B. Translated by Father Collins.

Life of Venerable Father Eudes. Translated from the French by Rev. Father Collins. Demy 18mo, ornamental cloth binding, price 6d.

www.ingramcontent.com/pod-product-compliance
Lightning Source LLC
Chambersburg PA
CBHW030052170426
43197CB00010B/1493